SCHIRMER'S LIBRARY
OF MUSICAL CLASSICS

Vol. 217

MAX BRUCH

Op. 26

Concerto

In G minor

For the Violin

With Piano Accompaniment

Edited and Fingered by

HENRY SCHRADIECK

G. SCHIRMER, Inc.

DISTRIBUTED BY

HAL•LEONARD®
CORPORATION

7777 W. BLUEMOUND RD. P.O. BOX 13819 MILWAUKEE, WI 53213

Concerto.

I. Prelude.

Edited and fingered by
Henry Schradieck.

MAX BRUCH. Op. **26**.

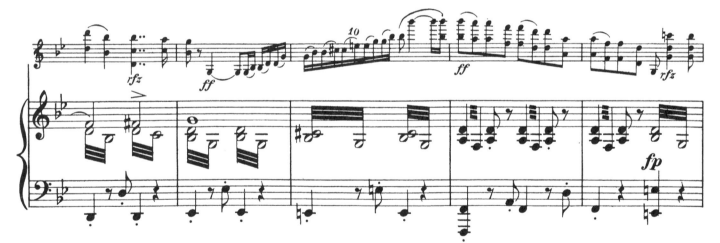

Un poco più lento.

Un poco più lento.

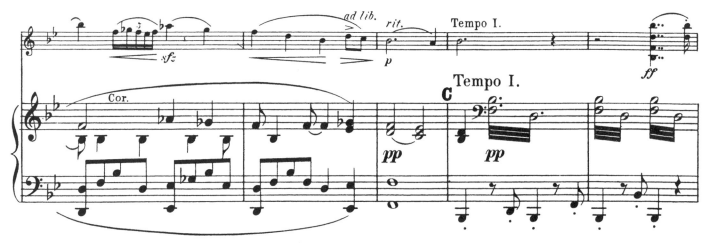

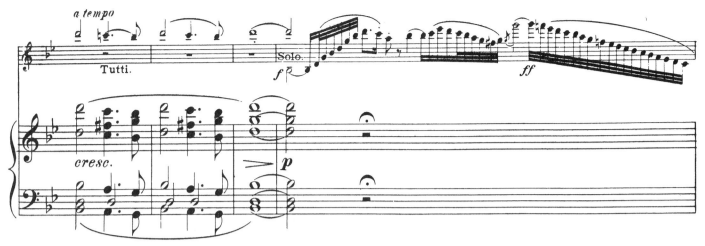

II. Adagio.

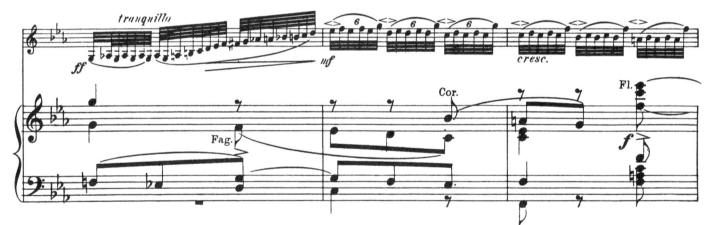

Concerto
I. Prelude.

Edited and fingered by
Henry Schradieck.

Violin.

MAX BRUCH. Op. **26.**

Violin.

II. Adagio.

Violin.

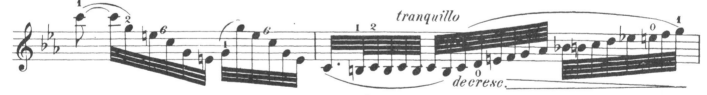

8

Violin.

10 Violin.

Violin.

12

Violin.

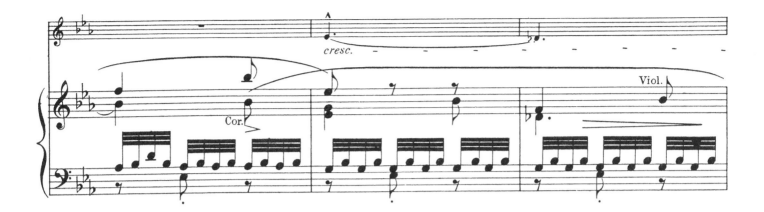

III. Finale.

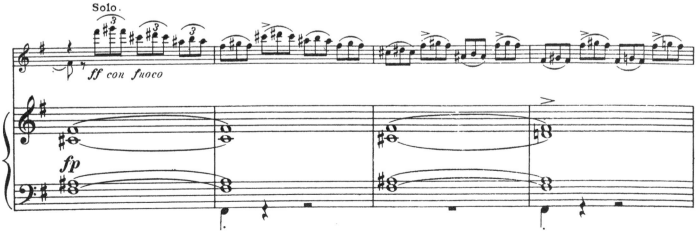

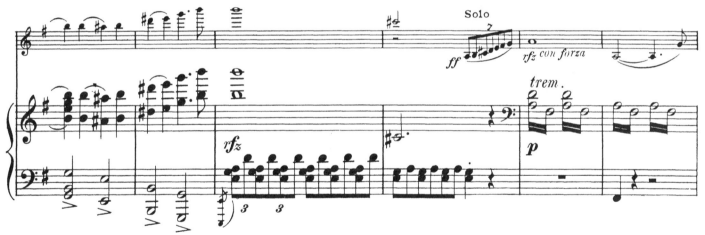

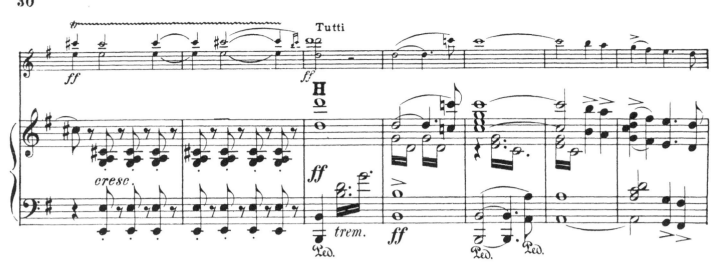

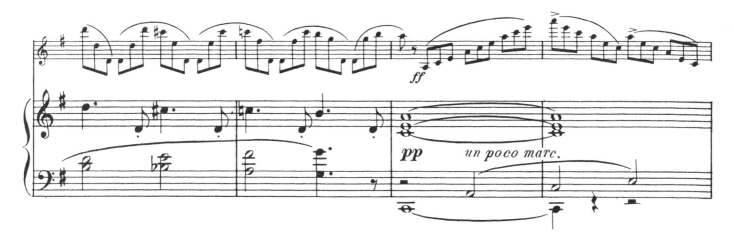

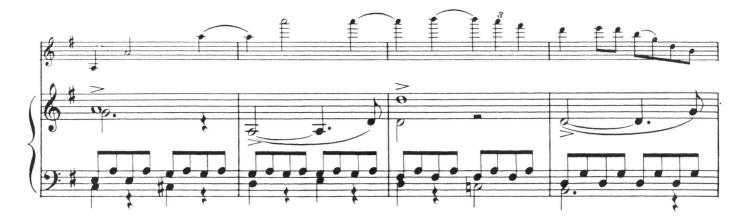

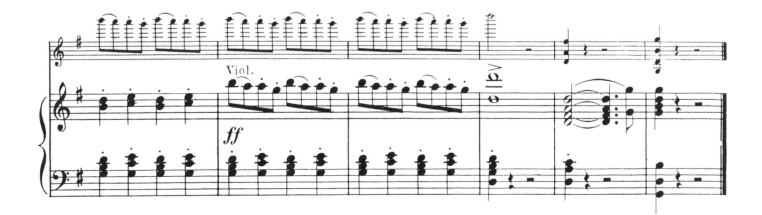